Bacteria

Staph, Strep, Clostridium,
and Other Bacteria

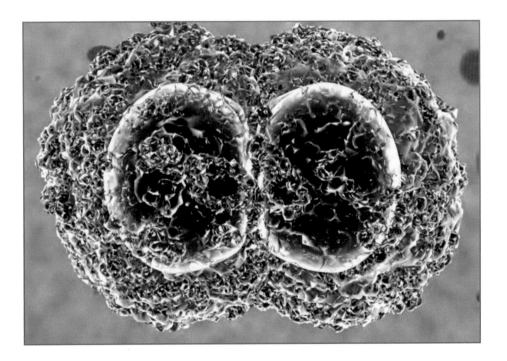

By
Judy Wearing

Crabtree Publishing Company

www.crabtreebooks.com

Crabtree Publishing Company

www.crabtreebooks.com

Author: Judy Wearing
Series consultant: Sally Morgan, MA, MSc, MIBiol
Project director: Ruth Owen
Designer: Alix Wood
Editors: Mark Sachner, Adrianna Morganelli
Proofreader: Crystal Sikkens
Project manager: Kathy Middleton
Print and production coordinator: Katherine Berti
Prepress technician: Katherine Berti

Production coordinated by Ruby Tuesday Books Ltd

Front cover: Computer artwork of *Escherichia coli*,
or *E. coli* for short, bacteria

Title page: Artwork of methicillin- (or multidrug-)
resistant *Staphyloccus aureus* (MRSA) showing
the bacteria's protective gel-like, or "slime," capsule

Photographs:
Alamy: page 20
FLPA: pages 13, 19, 37 (main), 38
Getty Images: page 43
International Medical Corps: page 36
Press Association Images: page 12
Ruby Tuesday Books Ltd: pages 6 (top), 14, 18, 28
Science Photo Library: front cover, pages 5 (all), 7, 11, 15 (all),
    17, 21, 24, 25, 27 (main), 29 (inset), 31, 32, 34, 40, 41, 42
Shutterstock: pages 1, 8, 9, 10, 23, 27 (inset), 29 (main), 30,
    33, 35 (main), 39
UNICEF: page 26
Wikipedia: pages 6 (bottom left), 6 (bottom right), 22 (all),
    35 (inset), 37 (inset)

Library and Archives Canada Cataloguing in Publication

Wearing, Judy
    Bacteria : staph, strep, clostridium, and other
bacteria / Judy Wearing.

(A class of their own)
Includes index.
ISBN 978-0-7787-5374-2 (bound).--ISBN 978-0-7787-5388-9 (pbk.)

    1. Bacteria--Classification--Juvenile literature.
2. Bacteria--Juvenile literature. I. Title.
II. Series: Class of their own

QR81.W42 2010   j579.301'2   C2009-907487-7

Library of Congress Cataloging-in-Publication Data

Wearing, Judy.
 Bacteria : staph, strep, clostridium, and other bacteria / by Judy Wearing.
    p. cm. -- (A class of their own)
 Includes index.
 ISBN 978-0-7787-5374-2 (reinforced lib. bdg. : alk. paper) -- ISBN 978-0-7787-
5388-9 (pbk. : alk. paper)
 1. Bacteria--Juvenile literature. I. Title. II. Series.

 QR74.8.W43 2010
 579.3--dc22

                                2009051394

Crabtree Publishing Company

www.crabtreebooks.com   1-800-387-7650

Printed in Canada / 052022 / CPC20220513

Published in Canada
Crabtree Publishing
616 Welland Ave.
St. Catharines, Ontario
L2M 5V6

Published in the United States
Crabtree Publishing
347 Fifth Ave
Suite 1402-145
New York, NY 10016

Published in the United Kingdom
Crabtree Publishing
Maritime House
Basin Road North, Hove
BN41 1WR

Published in Australia
Crabtree Publishing
Unit 3-5
Currumbin Court
Capalaba QLD 4157

Contents

WHAT ARE BACTERIA?

Bacteria are found everywhere, from tropical rain forests to mountaintops, from the frozen poles to boiling water, and in the deepest oceans. They live in our homes, on our skin, and inside our bodies. Bacteria are the most numerous organisms on Earth.

Ancient Life

Bacteria are tiny organisms with one cell. They are so small that as many as one million of them fit on the head of a pin. Powerful microscopes are needed to see them.

Bacteria are classified among living things in a *domain* of their own because the structure of their single cell is unlike that of animals, plants, and fungi. Bacteria cells are prokaryotic.

CASE STUDY

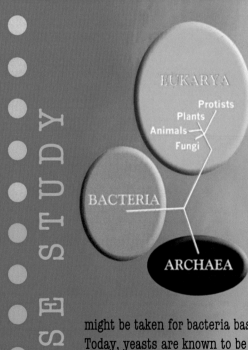

Kingdom or Domain?

The way life-forms are grouped, or classified, is constantly changing. Traditionally, organisms were classified as either animal or plant. Over the years, many organisms have been grouped *alongside* animals and plants, rather than *within* those two groups. For years, the classification of living things has been based on six *kingdoms* of life—animals, plants, fungi, protists, bacteria, and archaea.

As scientists improve their understanding of the genetic makeup of living things, they can better compare organisms. This understanding has helped scientists figure out even more detailed groupings of living things. In the past, organisms were grouped according to their appearance. Appearances can be misleading, however. Two organisms may look similar, but their genetic makeup can be very different. For example, some yeasts might be taken for bacteria based on the fact that, like bacteria, they consist of a single round cell. Today, yeasts are known to be fungi, not bacteria.

Some scientists now believe that organisms should be classified using an even bigger grouping than kingdom. This level is called the *domain*. These scientists propose that life should be divided into three domains—Eukarya, Bacteria, and Archaea. Within the domain Eukarya are the four kingdoms of animals, plants, fungi, and protists. These kingdoms are more closely related to each other than to the domains of bacteria and archaea.

This is where things stand—for now. As scientists continue to make new discoveries, this system will undoubtedly turn out to be another chapter in the story of life!

This means that they do not have a defined nucleus with a membrane around it. In fact, they do not have a membrane surrounding any of their cell parts. In contrast, plants, animals, and fungi are eukaryotic, which means that their cells have a membrane around the nucleus. The domain in which all plants, animals, and fungi are now classified is called Eukarya.

Prokaryotic cells are the simplest of cells. They were the first kind of cell on Earth. Bacteria have been around on Earth for about three billion years. Today there are vast numbers of species, perhaps as many as one billion. Scientists have only managed to describe 4,500 of them.

One reason bacteria are so hard to study is their size. Another reason is that many species cannot be grown in the laboratory, where scientists can study them.

Cross-sections of cells viewed through a scanning electron microscope (SEM)

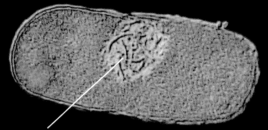

Prokaryotic bacterial cell with the genetic material lying in the cytoplasm

Eukaryotic cell from a mammal with a prominent nucleus surrounded by a membrane

A close-up of a section of a human tongue showing the bacteria (yellow strands) responsible for causing halitosis, or bad breath. Without a scanning electron microscope (SEM) it would not be possible to see the bacteria.

Good or Bad?

Many people think of bacteria as harmful because they cause food poisoning and diseases such as tuberculosis and anthrax. Most bacteria are not harmful, however. Many are incredibly important. As decomposers, they break down dead and rotting plants and animals. They help make soil, and they help plants grow.

The bacteria that live all over animals, including humans, help defend against disease. The species that live in the guts of animals—again, including humans—help break down food and produce vitamins. Bacteria are used to make some foods, as well as some medicines and vitamins. Bacteria are also used to clean up pollution.

Putting Bacteria in Groups: Shapes and Stains

Like all traditional classifications of living organisms, bacteria have been put into groups based on their appearance. Bacteria have several distinct cell shapes. Some are rod shaped, some round, and some spiral shaped. There are also curved rods, which look like macaroni, and thread-like bacteria.

The shape of bacteria is not enough to tell them apart. For example, there are thousands of rod-shaped bacteria. Many have the same size and shape, but some cause disease and some do not. The scientist Hans Christian Gram found one way to tell many bacteria apart—by looking at their cell walls.

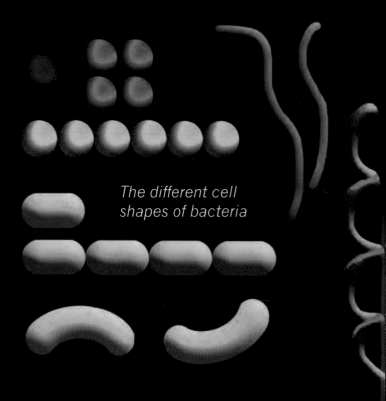

The different cell shapes of bacteria

Gram-negative bacteria

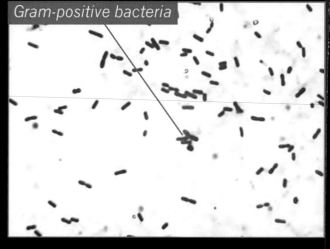

Gram-positive bacteria

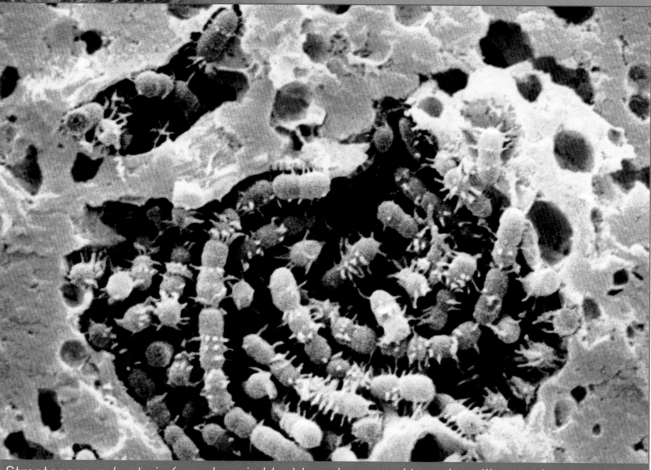

Streptococcus *bacteria (seen here in blue) have been used to make milk coagulate to produce goat cheese (the yellowish substance). As a gram-positive bacterium,* Streptococcus *stains purplish. In this computer-enhanced photo, the bacteria are shown as blue.*

In 1884, he soaked bacteria in crystal violet dye. Under the microscope, he noticed that the bacteria fell into two distinct groups: those with cell walls that were stained by the dye and those with cell walls that were not. The stained bacteria species were purplish; the unstained bacteria species were pink.

In this way, Gram was able to distinguish different species of bacteria that were exactly the same size and shape. This test, called gram staining, is often the first step in identifying bacteria. Bacteria that stain purplish (known as gram-positive bacteria) include *Streptococcus*, the cause of strep throat. Gram-negative bacteria, which only stain pink, have a coating of fat on their cell walls that prevents the dye from soaking in.

In more recent times, scientists have been reorganizing groups of bacteria based on their genes rather than shape and cell walls. This is resulting in big changes. The new system is still changing and is much more complex. Therefore, the bacteria groups in this book are based on the traditional groupings of shape and cell walls, rather than the classification systems used to group animals and plants (*kingdom, phylum/division, class, order,* and *family*), which reflect genetic similarity and are less likely to change. Although this does not reflect how bacteria are related by their genes, it does provide an excellent view of the variety of bacteria and their lifestyles.

CHAPTER ONE

THE BIOLOGY OF BACTERIA

One obvious feature of bacteria is their small size. On average, a bacterium is about two micrometers in length or diameter. That means that a teaspoon of soil can contain as many as one billion of them. Our bodies carry around ten bacteria cells for every one of our own human cells.

The Nature of Bacteria Cells

Bacteria cells are much simpler than those of plants or animals, so even though they are so small, their structure has been well studied. Scientists know that the cells of bacteria are also similar to the cells of other organisms in some basic ways. They all have a cell wall, nutrient storage areas, and DNA (the material containing the information that determines an organism's features).

There are also many differences between bacteria cells and those of other life-forms. With the exception of the domain Archaea, all life-forms other than bacteria are eukaryotic—that is, they have a membrane around the nucleus that separates the genetic material from the rest of the cell. Like Archaea, bacteria cells are prokaryotic, which means they lack a membrane around a nucleus and other inner cell parts.

This artwork shows a Salmonella *bacterium with many flagella.*

Most bacteria only have one string of DNA, which is arranged in a large, twisted loop. Plants and animals, in contrast, have several strings of DNA. Most bacteria also have extra, loose bits of DNA floating in their cells. Some of these bits—plasmids, are small and circular. They usually contain instructions that are beneficial to the makeup of the organism, but not necessary for survival.

Simply Amazing

Bacteria cells may be simple, but there are some amazing features among them. Some species trap gases in their cells and use the "bubble" to float or sink in water. Other bacteria collect a magnetic mineral in their cell. These bacteria use the mineral to sense magnetic fields. The benefit of this for the bacterium is a mystery.

Many bacteria have one or more flagella. These long, whip-like hairs allow bacteria to "swim." Flagella rotate like a propeller, by a wheel-like structure inside the cell wall. Many of the bacteria that cause disease have flagella. Some other, gram-negative bacteria (those that do not retain the purple gram stain used to identify bacteria) are covered by thin hairs. These hairs, called fimbriae, help the bacteria stick to things, including cells of plants and animals they infect.

Artwork showing E. coli *bacteria*

Flagellum

Fimbriae

HOW SMALL IS THAT?

How small are bacteria? They are almost too small to imagine, but here are some numbers. A micrometer is one-millionth of a meter, so there are one million micrometers in a meter, or 1,000 micrometers in a millimeter. To put it yet one more way, there are 25,000 micrometers in an inch. So at an average diameter or length of two micrometers, at least 500 bacteria would line up side by side in a millimeter, and 12,500 would line up in an inch!

Salinibacter ruber: The Salt Lover

For thousands of years, people have mined salt from the sea. They do this by making ponds along the coast with seawater in them. The water evaporates, leaving the salt behind. These salt ponds are some of the saltiest places on Earth.

Very little can survive in such salty conditions. Cells need water, and salt pulls water out of cells. There are, however, a few unique organisms that can live in these places. *Salinibacter ruber* is one of them. Discovered in 2000 in salt ponds in Spain, this bacterium is a halophile, or salt lover (*halo* means "salt"; *phile* means "like"). The rod-shaped bacterium is bright red and makes salt ponds a rusty color. To survive the salt, the bacterium has very high concentrations of potassium inside its cell. This prevents water from leaving the cell. The discovery of *Salinibacter ruber* was a surprise to scientists, who thought that only members of the domain Archaea could live in such conditions. While completely unrelated, *Salinibacter ruber* and archaea halophiles use the same strategies to survive in high salt. Some scientists think that the two groups of organisms got these abilities by sharing DNA at some point in the past!

Evaporated salt fields

Bacteria Habitats: Going to Extremes

All animals need oxygen to survive, but only some bacteria do. The species that use oxygen to produce usable energy are aerobic. Those that do not require oxygen are anaerobic, and they use other molecules to produce energy instead. The ability to survive where there is no oxygen is one reason that bacteria are found in so many places that other organisms are not.

Most bacteria live in relatively mild temperatures—above freezing (32°F or 0°C) to what would be considered a "high" human body temperature (104°F or 40°C). There are, however, a few species that live in temperatures as low as 14°F (-10°C) and as high as 221°F (105°C). This is hotter than boiling water. Bacteria have been discovered living in the presence of extreme chemicals as well, such as strong acids that destroy the cells of most other organisms.

Survival Tactics

A few species of bacteria have the ability to convert their cell into an endospore, which is a survival capsule in which the cell's activity slows down and becomes dormant. *Endo* means "inner"—as the spore is formed within the bacterium. This small, thick-walled spore can survive extreme conditions. Endospores can survive being dried out and exposed to cold, heat, and harmful UV (ultraviolet) rays from the Sun. When conditions are good for growth, the endospore will grow into a regular cell again.

Endospores can survive a very long time. Bacteria that produce endospores cause some of the worst diseases in humans: anthrax, botulism, gangrene, and tetanus. Endospores are the toughest of all life-forms and the oldest living organisms on Earth.

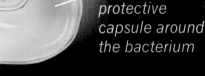

Gel-like protective capsule around the bacterium

SAFETY IN SLIME

Many bacteria are surrounded by a kind of capsule, a thick layer made of protein or mucous (slime). This layer protects the bacterium. Bacteria with slime capsules are more difficult for our immune system to kill should they invade our bodies. These capsules also give bacteria the ability to stick to things, so they can stick to the outside of a cell, or a place with a lot of food. Slime coatings and capsules protect bacteria from viruses and prevent them from drying out. The artwork above shows Haemophilus influenzae bacteria. This species causes bacterial meningitis and epiglottitis in children.

CASE STUDY

Bacillus permians:
The World's Oldest Living Organism?

Deep below the surface of a desert in New Mexico, researchers found endospores inside 250 million-year-old salt crystals. The researchers took the endospores and grew them in the laboratory. The researchers thought the endospores were trapped in the salt when the crystals were formed, 250 million years ago. This would make them the oldest-living organisms on Earth. They named the bacterium *Bacillus permians*. Other scientists believe that the bacterium found in the salt crystal is a very close relative of *Salibacillus marismortui*, a modern species that lives in salty places. They think the bacteria entered the salt crystal in recent times.

It is unlikely that *Bacillus permians* is 250 million years old, because DNA breaks apart over time. Once DNA in an endospore breaks apart, the bacterium is no longer alive. It cannot grow. Researchers studying the frozen ground of the Arctic used another way to figure out how old endospores can be. They looked for whole pieces of DNA, which indicate they came from organisms that were alive. They searched for the DNA of live organisms in soils that were up to one million years old. They found live bacteria cells that were 500,000 years old, but no older.

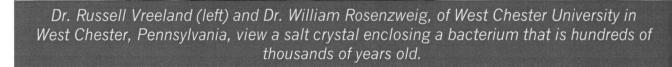

Dr. Russell Vreeland (left) and Dr. William Rosenzweig, of West Chester University in West Chester, Pennsylvania, view a salt crystal enclosing a bacterium that is hundreds of thousands of years old.

How Bacteria Get Food: Autotrophs and Heterotrophs

Bacteria get their food in many different ways. Some make their own sugars for energy, much as plants do. These bacteria are autotrophs. To do this, some use energy from the Sun as well as carbon dioxide and water. Other autotrophic bacteria use energy from the Sun, but instead of water they use hydrogen sulfide gas (the same gas responsible for the rotten egg smell). A few bacteria use carbon dioxide and water, but instead of energy from the Sun, they use energy from breaking down nitrogen or sulfur.

Other bacteria are heterotrophs. They get their energy by feeding on other organisms. Bacteria that feed on dead organisms are called saprotrophs. These bacteria are important for decomposing dead plants and animals. Decomposing is important because it puts nutrients back into soil and water for other organisms to use.

Some bacteria live in close relationships with other organisms. Mutualists live with other species to the benefit of both. One group of important bacterial mutualists are species in the genus *Rhizobium*. These bacteria live in small lumps on the roots of plants in the pea, bean, and alfalfa family. The *Rhizobium* provides the plant with nitrogen. Nitrogen is required to make proteins and DNA. Plants have a shortage of nitrogen, because even though 80 percent of air is nitrogen gas, plants and animals cannot use it. Plants can only use nitrogen that has hydrogen added to it. *Rhizobium* adds hydrogen to nitrogen gas and makes it usable by the plant. In exchange for this "nitrogen fixation," the plant gives *Rhizobium* nutrients. *Rhizobium*, as well as other bacteria that live in soil and water, produce 60 percent of the nitrogen used by organisms to grow. Without these bacteria, there would be a lot less life on the planet.

Some bacteria are parasites. They live with others in relationships that benefit the bacteria but harm the other organism. Bacteria that cause disease are parasites.

Rhizobium *nodules on the roots of a broad bean*

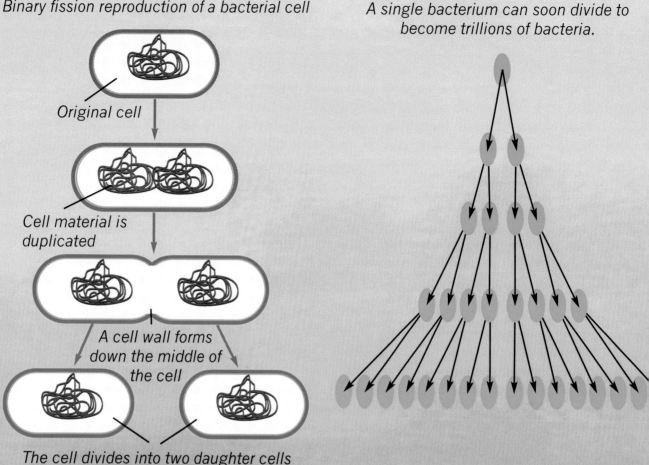

Binary fission reproduction of a bacterial cell

Original cell

Cell material is duplicated

A cell wall forms down the middle of the cell

The cell divides into two daughter cells

A single bacterium can soon divide to become trillions of bacteria.

Growing and Dividing: How Bacteria Reproduce

Bacteria reproduce asexually by making copies of themselves. Most bacteria do this by binary fission (*binary* means "two"; *fission* means "split"). A bacteria cell grows and copies its DNA and cell contents. Then it makes a cell wall down the middle to divide the cell contents into two separate cells. Instead of one cell, there are now two identical daughter cells. In nature, it takes some bacteria 15 minutes to grow and divide and others as long as many days. The new bacteria also grow and divide. In this way, bacteria increase in number very quickly. A single bacterium that divides every 15 minutes can become a population of 300 trillion in 12 hours!

Exchanging and Sharing Genes

Most organisms, including plants, animals, and fungi, reproduce sexually. Two individuals com together, combine their DNA, and then form new individuals that contain a mixture of DNA from both parents. Bacteria share their DNA, too, but they do this without reproduction, so no new individuals are formed. One way bacteria share their genes is to join with another bacterium. Some touch cell walls together and form a bridge between them. Others grow a tube that is inserted into another bacterium.

When two bacteria are joined, DNA from one individual is copied. The copy might be a plasmid (a small, loose bit of DNA in the cell) or a section of DNA from the nucleus. The copy is then "given" to the other bacterium. The new DNA becomes either a plasmid or a part of the bacterium's nucleus. When this bacterium reproduces, both daughter cells will have the new DNA. In this way, genes from one individual bacterium can become common throughout an entire population of bacteria.

Bacteria pick up new DNA from other sources, too. If they feed on a dead bacterium, bits of the DNA they digest can be included in their nucleus or stay inside the cell. If the new DNA is put into the nucleus, or is a complete plasmid, it will be replicated and passed on to daughter cells. (If the DNA is only a bit of a plasmid, it will not be replicated and passed on.) In this way, bacteria regularly mix up their genes and gain new characteristics. Some new characteristics will provide bacteria with the means to survive, and some new characteristics will not.

Bacteria with a tube, called a pilus, to transfer genetic material between cells.

Two cells with a mating bridge sharing DNA

How Bacteria Gene Sharing Affects Us

Thanks to their ability to share and pick up DNA from other sources, bacteria are able to adapt quickly to changing conditions. Some bacteria that cause disease develop ways to overcome medicines used to kill them. The ability to survive poisons is known as resistance. Resistance in one bacterium can be shared, and spread, to other bacteria in a population.

The exchange of DNA between bacteria also makes it difficult for scientists to use DNA to classify them. DNA from more than one species often exists in a single bacterium. For this reason, bacteria are classified using another material that is, like DNA, a nucleic acid. This material is found in other parts of the cell, called ribosomes, which is where proteins are made. The material is known as ribosomal RNA, or rRNA.

Manipulating Genes:
Bacteria in Technology

Bacteria are very useful to humans. For one thing, they have made genetic engineering possible. This new science involves changing the genes of organisms for human benefit.

One example of genetic engineering is the use of bacteria to make human insulin, a hormone humans need to use food for energy. People with diabetes do not have enough insulin. They need to add insulin to their blood stream every day. It took a lot of research to work out the mechanics, but bacteria have been the main source of human insulin since the 1980s.

First, scientists changed the human DNA so it would "work" when it is put into a bacterium. To do this, they remove a bacterium's plasmid, cut it, put the human DNA for making insulin into it, and connect the plasmid again. Then they make copies of the plasmid and introduce it to other bacteria cells. Any bacteria that take up the plasmid produce insulin. Once the plasmid is established in the other bacteria, that plasmid also gets passed down to daughter cells. In a short time, millions of bacteria producing insulin can be grown. This technology has made insulin easy to get, and it has saved lives. Scientists cannot tell the difference between the insulin made by humans and the insulin made by the bacteria.

There are many other examples of bacteria being used in genetic engineering. In agriculture, it is common to put genes from bacteria into crops. Some added genes cause the plant to produce a chemical that kills insects, make the plant last longer before it rots, or make the plant more nutritious. New uses for genetic engineering continue to be found, but some people are worried. They say that the results of changing DNA are unknown. They wonder if genes will jump from one organism to another or destroy the balance of life.

HOW GENETIC ENGINEERING WORKS

The first step of genetic engineering is to isolate and identify genes from an organism that have some benefit (such as the ability to produce insulin). Then, the genes are altered so the wanted characteristic will also be produced in a new organism. Copies of the genes are made, and then they are put into a new organism. The new organism will have the wanted characteristic. Genes are the instructions for everything an organism does, from making a molecule to making organs and whole organisms. The possibilities of what genetic engineering can do are endless.

Genetically modified corn with dead weeds below. The corn has been engineered to be resistant to the herbicide used to kill the weeds. Reducing competition from weeds will increase crop yields.

CHAPTER TWO

BACILLI: ROD-SHAPED BACTERIA

A typical rod-shaped bacterium is shaped like a vitamin capsule: a c
rounded ends. There are many variations, however. They can be
and long or short; have pointed or rounded ends; be curved or str
m-negative or gram-positive. Some require oxygen to live and are aer
not require oxygen and are anaerobic.

gles, Chains, and Chinese Letters: Bacilli Arrangements

-shaped bacteria are found in nature in several arrangements. Some live singl
found in a chain of cells attached end to end, like a string of sausages. Some
and at angles to each other in an arrangement that resembles Chinese letters
oduction, rod-shaped bacteria divide down the middle of the cylinder, not len
the pattern of reproduction that determines the arrangement.

Bacilli

Streptobacilli *showing chain arrangement*

Bacilli *showing palisade ar*

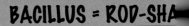

BACILLI: THE SMITH AND JONES OF BACTERIA

If the world of bacteria had a phone book, there
would be many listings under "Bacillus" (singular)
and "Bacilli" (plural)! These are like common
names that are seen in a lot of places. The term
"bacilli" refers to all bacteria that are rod-
shaped. It also refers to a specific group of
bacteria, the class Bacilli—some of which are
rod-shaped and some of which are not. There is
also a smaller group, which is also very specific,
the genus Bacillus, whose species are all
rod-shaped.

BACILLUS = ROD-SHA

The word "bacillus" in the sc
of a bacterium is a guarante
rod-shaped. Not all rod-shap
have "bacillus" in their scier
however. For example, Fusob
polymorphum is a bacillus, b

Bacteria that live singly are bacilli. After binary fission, the daughter cells separate. Bacteria with the chain type of arrangement are called streptobacilli. With chains of rod-shaped bacteria, reproduction adds more "sausages" to the end of the string. Bacteria with the third type of arrangement are called palisade. They exist in side-by-side stacks or at sharp angles to each other. This arrangement occurs in species in which the dividing cell wall "snaps" apart, leaving the two daughter cells touching one another at an angle, or stacked up side by side.

Lab Rats, Hot Springs, and Disease: *Bacillus* Species

The genus *Bacillus* includes species that are commonly found in the environment, particularly in soil. Some live in hot temperatures and are found in hot springs. Of all the *Bacillus* species, many are harmless, some are beneficial, and a few are harmful. All of them require oxygen, are gram-positive, and make endospores. There are several *Bacillus* species used in industry. Some are used in making antibiotics. Others make proteins used in detergents, agriculture, and the food industry. Others are used to kill insects such as mosquitoes or crop pests. One species, *Bacillus subtilis*, is the bacterial equivalent of a "lab rat." It is used by scientists to study cells and DNA.

Among the bacilli are some species of bacteria that thrive in temperatures as hot as 212°F (100°C). This hot spring in Yellowstone National Park, Wyoming, is home to dozens of bacteria, some of which are brightly colored.

Bacillus anthracis causes anthrax, a deadly disease that affects cattle, sheep, and people. Anthrax spreads when an animal, or person, comes into contact with an infected animal. Eating meat from an infected animal can also cause anthrax, as can coming into contact with the endospores. The endospores survive in the soil for years, and if a person accidentally eats or breathes them in, he or she can get the disease. If this happens, there's a good chance the victim will die.

Industry, "Green" Fuel, and Gangrene: *Clostridium* Species

Clostridium is a genus of gram-positive, rod-shaped bacteria that live in environments where there is no oxygen. These bacteria form endospores. They are found in soils, in lake sediments, and in the guts of animals. There are about 100 species of *Clostridium*. Of those, several have been used in industry. Since 1916, *Clostridium acetobutylicum* has been used to make acetone and butanol. These two chemicals are important for making gunpowder, the explosive TNT, and car finishes, among other things. Another species helps make plastic, glue, antifreeze, and paint. Two species of *Clostridium* are being studied and used to make ethanol. Ethanol is an alternative fuel for cars.

A BIOLOGICAL WEAPON

Because anthrax spores are microscopic, do not dry out, and are so deadly, they have been used as a weapon. Breathing in the spores leads to the most deadly form of the disease. Symptoms of anthrax include fever and tiredness. Within one to two days, difficulty breathing and shock can result in death. In 2001, anthrax spores were mailed in envelopes by a terrorist in the United States to TV newsrooms and government offices. When the victims of the attack opened the envelopes, they breathed in the spores. Five people died in the attack.

Anthrax clean-up workers rinse off after exiting the Hart Senate Office Building in Washington, D.C. The building was contaminated by anthrax in a letter sent to Senate Majority Leader Tom Daschle.

While it is a small portion of rod-shaped bacteria species that cause disease, the ones that do get a lot of attention. Despite all its positive uses, *Clostridium* is best known for species that cause humans harm. They cause the diseases tetanus, botulism, and gangrene. These bacteria do not need oxygen and are thus able to live inside animal bodies. Because they form endospores, they are also able to survive outside the body in a dormant state. This gives the bacteria a way to spread from person to person. People who make contact with the spores in the environment can become infected.

Tetanus

Tetanus is the disease caused by *Clostridium tetani.* This bacterium's spores are found in soil. They can get into a wound if they come into contact with broken skin, perhaps if someone steps on an old nail in the soil. The new bacterial cells will then grow from the spores. The bacterium grows in the region of the wound and makes one of the most poisonous substances produced by any organism. The poison travels up the nerves, causing muscles to jerk and "lock." The locking of muscles gives the disease its common name: "lockjaw." Each year, more than 300,000 people get tetanus, or lockjaw, around the world, but very few cases occur in North America. Almost all cases occur in people who have not been properly immunized, or vaccinated, against the disease. One half to three-quarters of people who get tetanus die from it.

A Clostridium tetani bacterial endospore that causes tetanus

The endospore has developed a thick outer wall of many membranes (the purple layers).

The bacterium Yersinia pestis

This painting, entitled The Triumph of Death, *by Dutch artist Pieter Bruegel, shows the horror and devastation of the Black Death in medieval Europe.*

Yersinia pestis: The Black Death

Between 1340 and 1353, one-third of all the people in Europe died in an onslaught of disease known as the Black Death. Villages became ghost towns, animals were left without farmers to feed them, and bodies were piled high in city streets. The cause of the destruction was a rod-shaped bacterium, *Yersinia pestis* (called *Y. pestis* for short), which results in the disease bubonic plague. People are not the main host of this deadly parasite. Rats are. When rat fleas with *Y. pestis* feed on rats, the bacteria enter the rats. Those rats get sick, and many die. When fleas that have *Y. pestis* feed on humans, the disease can be given to humans as well. Large numbers of human deaths occur when large numbers of rats are killed by the disease, and their hungry fleas look for food elsewhere.

Bubonic plague involves fever, exhaustion, and painful swellings in the armpits and other places on the body. The disease kills by destroying the immune system. Before antibiotics, the plague killed nearly 100 percent of the people it infected. Today, one in seven people in the United States who get the disease die.

Botulism

Botulism is caused by *Clostridium botulinum.* This bacterium also makes a deadly poison. It grows naturally in soil, lake sediments, and rotting vegetables. If vegetables with this bacterium are eaten, the poison can really do harm. It stops nerves from working and prevents muscles from moving. The victim becomes paralyzed and dies if the muscles of the lungs and heart stop working. Without treatment, one in four people who get botulism die.

Botulism is rare, but when it does occur, it is usually because of tainted food from a jar or a can. Inside a can or sealed jar, there is food, but there is also no oxygen—not an environment in which most bacteria thrive, but just the right conditions for this bacterium to grow. If the jars or cans are not heated to a high enough temperature for a certain amount of time, endospores can grow and produce the poison. Cans of food that are swollen have gas in them. Since *Clostridium botulinum* produces gas, this is a sign the bacterium might be in the food. It should not be eaten.

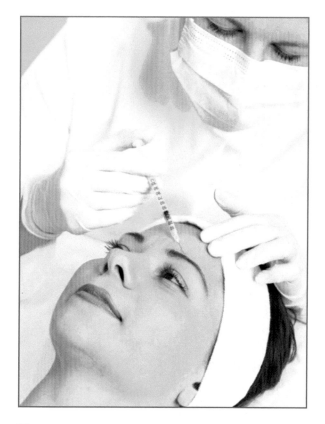

Though botulism toxin can kill a person who consumes it, it has found another use as a beauty aid. When a version of the toxin, Botox, is injected into the forehead, it paralyzes the muscles and prevents frown lines. The effect lasts several months.

Gangrene

Clostridium perfringens (*C. perfringens* for short) can cause gangrene. Gangrene happens when tissues of the body die and rot. Gangrene can have several causes, but one of them is the growth of this bacterium. After surgery or a wound, if this bacterium is present, it can feed on the flesh and produce poisons. It also makes gases while it lives and grows. Gangrene caused by *C. perfringens* is known as gas gangrene because bubbles of gas form under the skin. The poison produced by *C. perfringens* can also cause food poisoning, usually in cans of food that have not been heated up properly. *C. perfringens* food poisoning is serious, but not as severe as botulism.

Living in the Gut: Rod-Shaped Bacteria in the Intestines

Our intestines are teeming with life. Bacteria are the most common residents, with about 500 to 1,000 different species living in our guts. About 60 percent of the weight of our feces is made up of bacteria cells.

Because there is no oxygen in our intestines, all intestinal bacteria are anaerobic. Many of these bacteria species have positive effects on us. A few species, however, cause us harm. Rod-shaped species are found in both the beneficial group and the harmful group. *Bifidobacterium longum* is a bacterium that has a positive effect. It helps our immune system and prevents harmful bacteria from making us sick. It also helps us break down sugars for nutrition. Another common species in our intestines, *Bacteriodes thetaiotaomicron*, helps us digest carbohydrates. It makes vitamins K and B. It also helps our immune system. This species makes up about 25 percent of the total bacteria cells in our intestines.

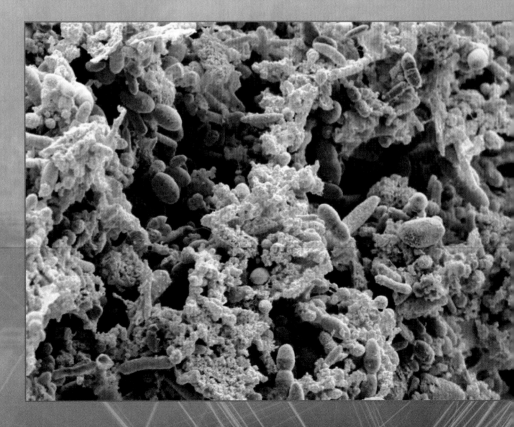

A colored scanning electron micrograph (SEM) showing the numbers of bacteria (pink) in human feces (gray)

There are a few rod-shaped bacteria living in our guts that can cause problems. The most famous of these is *Escherichia coli*, or *E. coli* for short. Most of the time, *E. coli* is helpful to us. It prevents harmful bacteria from becoming too numerous, and it makes vitamin K. Some types of *E. coli* can cause food poisoning, however. Drinking or eating water or food that has human feces in it can result in diarrhea and in some cases even death.

Salmonella is another famous gut bacterium. It is the second most common cause of food poisoning. This bacterium causes stomach cramps, diarrhea, and vomiting. Just 15 to 20 bacteria cells can result in illness. People become ill when they eat raw animal products that have some animal feces containing *Salmonella* on them. Any contact with animal feces, including that of pets, can lead to illness. To avoid *Salmonella* poisoning, wash your hands before and after making food. *Salmonella* is killed when food is cooked, so cooking eggs and meat products also prevents illness.

Fighting Back: Vaccines That Stop Bacteria

There is one advance in science that has prevented more deaths from bacteria diseases than any other: vaccination. To be vaccinated, a person is given, usually by a needle, a version of the bacterium (or virus) that causes illness. The bacterium that is injected has been changed in some way, however, so that it does not cause illness. The vaccine is made up of dead cells, or only part of the cells, or a version of the bacterium with its genes changed so it is harmless. In all cases, the vaccine protects the person who receives it from becoming ill from this bacterium in the future. The vaccine does this by causing the immune system to recognize the bacterium and create proteins that will destroy it.

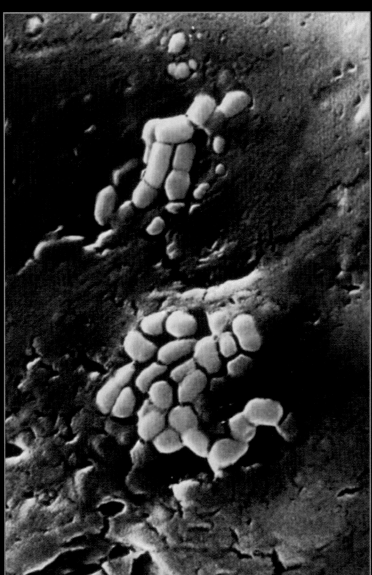

A colored scanning electron micrograph (SEM) of the surface of cooked roast beef (brown). Colonies of Salmonella *bacteria (green) are forming following a visit from a housefly carrying animal feces on its feet.*

If the bacterium that causes disease gets into a person's body at some time in the future, the immune system is ready. It will be able to quickly kill the bacterium before it can cause disease.

Most children in the United States and Canada get a vaccination called DPT. The letters stand for the diseases the vaccine guards against: diphtheria, pertussis (whooping cough), and tetanus. Different rod-shaped bacteria cause these three diseases. Diphtheria and pertussis are diseases of the breathing passages. They both spread quickly from person to person. Before the vaccine, both diseases killed thousands of people in North America every year, particularly young children. Today, there are only a few cases of these diseases every year. In countries where children are not vaccinated, deaths from diphtheria and pertussis are still common.

The same vaccine that protects against these bacteria also protects children from tetanus. Thousands of people still die from tetanus around the world each year, but few of these are in North America. This is because of the vaccine.

WEIGHING THE RISKS

Some parents are concerned that vaccines themselves may do harm to children. In rare cases, an allergic reaction or some other side effect may occur as a result of the vaccine. In the population as a whole—particularly among school-age children—the benefits of receiving vaccines far outweigh the risk of side effects. Meanwhile, scientists continue to improve vaccines to make them even safer.

During 2008–2009, the diaper manufacturer Pampers joined forces with UNICEF to launch a campaign called "One Pack = One Vaccine." For every pack of Pampers purchased, the cost of a tetanus vaccine is donated to UNICEF. The campaign aims to deliver 200 million tetanus vaccines to fight this disease in newborn babies and mothers-to-be (seen here) in developing countries.

Lactobacillus bulgaricus:
Yogurt and the Immune System

Yogurt is milk with bacteria added to it. The bacteria grow, multiply, and feed on the sugar in the milk. They make lactic acid in the process. Yogurt, the product of this process, is thick and creamy and has a tart taste. People have been making it for at least 4,500 years. Yogurt and the bacteria that grow and live in it are good for our bodies. Both *Lactobacillus bulgaricus* and *Lactobacillus acidophilus* (another rod-shaped bacterium used to make yogurt) make yogurt more nutritious than milk.

Yogurt is an excellent source of protein and B vitamins, and it is easily digested. The bacteria also seem to help people lose weight. They boost the immune system and keep other bacteria from doing harm. They are even thought to help prevent cancer and give people longer lives. People from countries such as Bulgaria, where yogurt has been a part of their diet for hundreds of years, live a long time and have few cases of stomach cancer.

Lactobacillus bulgaricus

Yogurt

27

CHAPTER THREE

COCCI: ROUND BACTERIA

Cocci are a group of bacteria whose cells have spherical or oval shapes. *Coccus* comes from *kokkos*, which is Greek for "berry." Cocci may be gram-negative and gram-positive, aerobic and anaerobic. The average size of a coccus bacterium is 0.5-1.0 micrometer in diameter. Most cocci have a positive or neutral effect on humans. Some, however, cause disease.

Balls, Chains, and Clusters: Cocci Arrangements

Many coccus bacteria occur in nature as single spheres. When other coccus bacteria reproduce, the cells stay together in particular arrangements that are specific to the species. Some species occur in pairs. Other coccus bacteria continue to reproduce, so a chain of daughter cells develops. This arrangement is typical of *Streptococcus*.

If a coccus undergoes binary fission in one direction, it becomes two "balls," side by side. Then each of those cells undergoes binary fission in the other direction, up and down, the result will be four cells in a square formation. If those four cells undergo binary fission again, a cube of eight cells can result.

Environmental Clean-Up

Using bacteria to clean up waste is common. Bacteria are being used to clean up human sewage and oil spills. They also help clean up pollution from heavy metals and industrial chemicals. More and more uses for clean-up bacteria are being found. These bacteria include bacilli and cocci, with certain species of cocci playing important roles. Experiments in the ocean near Japan have shown three main groups of bacteria that break down oil. All three of them are cocci: *Actinobacter* species, *Psychrobacter immobilis*, and another, unnamed group of cocci. Scientists continue to study these bacteria with the goal of using them to help clean up oil spills.

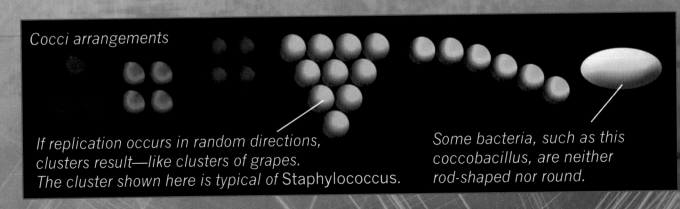

Cocci arrangements

If replication occurs in random directions, clusters result—like clusters of grapes. The cluster shown here is typical of Staphylococcus.

Some bacteria, such as this coccobacillus, are neither rod-shaped nor round.

One coccus species has an amazing ability to survive radiation from the Sun or from nuclear waste. This makes it useful for cleaning up some of the most difficult pollution. *Deinococcus radiodurans* is featured in the *Guinness Book of World Records* as the "world's toughest bacterium." It is gram-positive with an arrangement of four cocci in a "square." This bacterium has the ability to survive 1,000 times the amount of radiation that humans can. It can also survive being dried out. High acid levels and cold temperatures do not kill it, either.

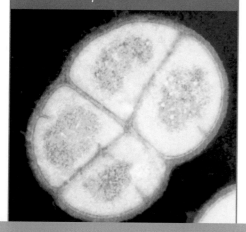

Deinococcus radiodurans, *known as the "world's toughest bacterium," is shown reproducing in a square formation.*

NEVER SAY DIE

Radiation destroys DNA. In a matter of hours after having its DNA destroyed by radiation, however, the Deinococcus radiodurans bacterium simply puts its bits of DNA back together. Being able to survive high radiation makes this bacterium able to live in areas where there are nuclear wastes. Scientists are using genetic engineering to put the "pollution-eating" genes of other bacteria into D. radiodurans. The result is a bacterium that both "eats" pollution and survives some of the worst conditions on Earth.

THE CHLORINE CLEANER

Chlorine is found in bleach. It is used in industry to clean water and to make plastics, paper, and batteries. It is poisonous to the environment and does harm to living things. Before the dangers were known, chlorine chemicals were dumped in the environment. They are now found in groundwater and soil in some areas. Removing chlorine is very difficult and expensive. In 2003, researchers discovered a bacterium that "eats" chlorine. Their studies found that the coccus Dehalococcoides ethenogenes breaks down chlorine chemicals into harmless substances.

An oil spill damaging the shore. Certain bacteria are able to break down oil and have been useful in cleaning up oil spills.

Cows and Their Stomachs: Mutualistic Cocci

Cows, sheep, and goats eat grass and hay and are able to break down the complex carbohydrate molecules in those plants. Actually, it is bacteria that live inside these animals that digest the plant's complex molecules for them. Many species of bacteria, particularly some cocci, live in special cavities in the digestive systems of these animals. Here, they process food before it gets to the animal's stomach. It is often said these animals have four stomachs. The main cavity where the bacteria live is called the rumen, and animals that have a rumen are called ruminants.

The bacteria benefit from this association with the animals, which is called a mutualistic relationship. They are provided with food and a place to live. The animals benefit from this relationship, too. They feed on the molecules that result from the bacteria breaking down the grass and hay. These molecules are absorbed into the blood from the rumen. They supply the animal with about three-quarters of its energy. The digestion of the rest of the food takes place in the stomach.

Human vs. Bacteria: The Battle to Stop Infection

About one-third of all bacterial infections are caused by gram-positive cocci. This group causes pneumonia, meningitis, strep throat, ear infections, skin infections, and blood infections. Though the bacteria in this group are not related by genetics, they have a similar lifestyle. They all are aerobic, which determines where they can live. Gram-positive cocci are among the most common bacteria that are found on human skin. They live in the lining of the nose, throat, and lungs.

The rumen of a cow can hold about 33 gallons (125 liters)

Most of these species do not harm us, but the few that do are difficult to kill. Their thick cell walls protect them from our immune system. A gram-positive cocci infection results in pus, a white or yellowish paste that contains dead bacteria and dead and live white blood cells. Pus is a sign that the body is working to protect itself.

Streptococcus

Streptococcus pneumoniae (*S. pneumoniae* for short) lives in the nose and throat of many people and usually does no harm. If, however, the immune system is weak, *S. pneumoniae* can begin to grow on tissues on which it does not normally thrive. The passages of the lungs, the ear canals, and the nervous system can all be affected. If this happens, disease can result. A bacterial infection in the lungs is called pneumonia. This causes a person to have difficulty breathing. *S. pneumoniae* is the leading cause of pneumonia.

A related species, *Streptococcus pyogenes* (*S. pyogenes*) is another common bacterium in the human nose and throat. It occurs in about 15 percent of people and does little harm. If the immune system is weak, however, *S. pyogenes* can replicate in such numbers that it causes disease. Strep throat is an infection of this bacterium in the throat. Fever and a very painful throat are the main symptoms. The bacterium can also infect wounds and cuts, and if it gains access to the bloodstream through a wound, it can be fatal. Tonsillitis, scarlet fever, and toxic shock syndrome are all the result of a *S. pyogenes* infection. *Streptococcus* infections are treated with antibiotics, which kill the cells and bring the number of bacteria under control.

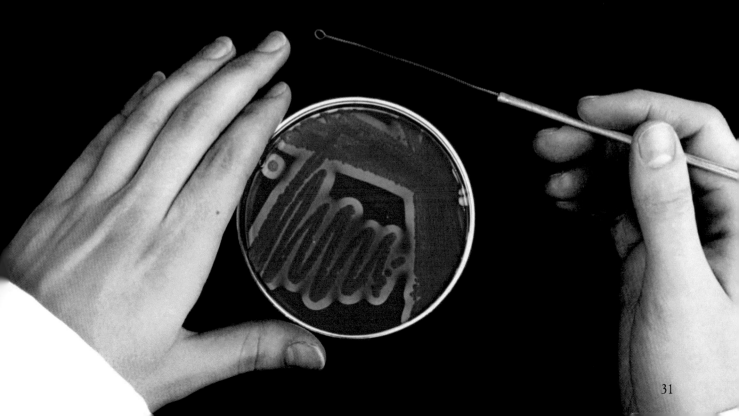

This researcher is using a metal loop to spread Streptococcus pyogenes *in a petri dish. The bacteria are growing on a mixture that contains red blood cells. The bacteria cause the blood cells to burst.*

Staphylococcus

Two species of *staphylococcus* are common residents of our skin: *Staphylococcus epidermidis* and *Staphylococcus aureus. S. epidermidis* is a beneficial guest that exists in large quantities. The acid it produces prevents unwanted fungi from growing on us. *S. aureus* is another story. It lives on 10 to 40 percent of our bodies, on our skin, in our noses, and in our intestines. Most of the time it does no harm. Some types of *S. aureus* feed on human cells, however, and cause health problems in the process. This bacterium can cause a wide variety of infections, commonly known as staph infections—from pimples and boils, to pneumonia and wound or blood infections—that can be fatal.

Streptococcus mutans and Friends: Plaque and Tooth Decay

Shortly after we brush our teeth, they start to become recoated by a layer of proteins and mucous from our saliva. Three species of bacteria appear soon afterward: *Streptococcus mutans*, a coccus, along with its relative *Streptococcus sanguis* and the rod-shaped *Actinomyces viscosus*. Proteins on the surface of these bacteria bind tightly to the proteins on our teeth. For several days, as long as the teeth are not brushed, the trio of bacteria multiplies on the surface. New bacteria species now have something to stick to. Eventually, a solid biofilm with as many as 400 different species forms. The bacteria in this biofilm are doing more than just sticking to each other. They are interacting. The different species share and trade nutrients. Dentists call the biofilm "plaque." It is very difficult to remove!

The trio of *Streptococcus* and *Actinomyces* species not only start plaque, but they also cause tooth decay. These bacteria feed on sugar and produce lactic acid in the process. The acid dissolves the surface of the teeth. Cavities are holes and cracks in the tooth's surface where the tooth has dissolved.

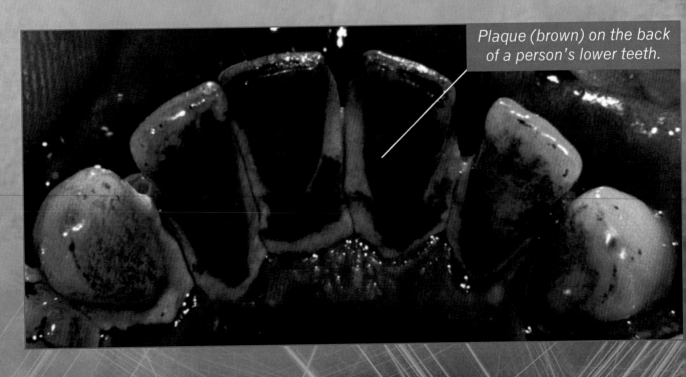

Plaque (brown) on the back of a person's lower teeth.

MRSAs: Antibiotic-Resistant Staph

Some bacteria, including some kinds of *S. aureus*, do not respond to treatment by common antibiotics. Antibiotics are chemicals that are poisonous to bacteria. They are the main strategy used in medicine to combat infection. Some bacteria, particularly some kinds of *S. aureus*, have developed the ability to survive these poisons. These bacteria are known as MRSAs, which stands for methicillin-resistant (or multidrug-resistant) *Staphyloccus aureus*.

These drug-resistant strains of *S. aureus* cause hospitals particular worry. They can infect the skin or other areas, and because they cannot be killed, they can result in serious illness. Resistant *S. aureus* strains are spreading and becoming more common. Resistance spreads easily because the gene that gives the bacterium this ability is located on a plasmid. Bacteria with the plasmid not only pass it down to their daughter cells but also share it with other *S. aureus*. Handwashing helps the situation, but it is not enough. *S. aureus* strains now exist that cannot be killed by any of the antibiotics we have. It is only a matter of time before this super resistance spreads. Meanwhile, certain compounds have been found to be more effective than others at fighting MRSAs, and scientists are battling to continue to develop new antibiotics to fight staph infections.

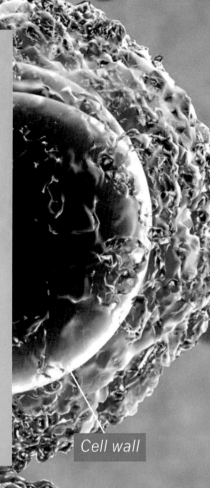

Cell wall

"Slime" capsule

Artwork of multidrug-resistant Staphyloccus aureus *(MRSA) showing the bacteria's protective gel-like or "slime" capsule.*

33

CHAPTER FOUR

CURVED BACTERIA: COMMAS AND SPIRALS

The third major shape of bacteria (in addition to round and rod-shaped) is the curve. The bacteria in this loose grouping can take several forms.

Twists and Turns

Slightly curved bacteria cells look like commas and are known as vibrios. They are gram-negative and many live in water, particularly the saltwater of the oceans. More tightly twisted bacteria cells form spirals, called spirilla. These bacteria have stiff cells, like dry pasta. They can be large by bacteria standards, in the region of one micrometer to about 100 micrometers. They are also gram-negative. A third form in this group has a looser spiral and more flexible cells. These cells are long and thin, and they look a little bit like party streamers. They are called spirochetes. Spirochetes are a unique group of bacteria that are related by their genes as well as similar in appearance. Most spirochetes live in mud or inside animals. A few species cause disease.

MOVEMENT IN CURVED BACTERIA

Many comma-shaped bacteria and spirilla have flagella at their ends. The flagella rotate and propel the bacteria forward. Spirochete flagella are unique. These flagella occur along the length of the bacterium, but they are enclosed! The flagella are contained in a space between the cell wall and an outer membrane. When the flagella turn and bend, the spirochete cell bends, twists, and moves like a corkscrew.

Diseases Caused by Curved Bacteria

There are several important diseases caused by curved species of bacteria. The spirochete *Borrelia burgdorferi* causes Lyme disease. This bacterium normally lives in mice and deer. It gets into humans when a deer tick feeds on the blood of a deer, picks up the bacterium, and then feeds on a human. The tick then transfers the bacterium from the deer to the human. Lyme disease is a recent discovery. It was first described in 1975. The disease was linked to the bacterium in the 1980s. The first sign of Lyme disease is a red rash around a tick bite. In the weeks afterward, tiredness, headaches, fever, and numbness can follow. Over months and years, arthritis, mental illness, or irregular heartbeat can occur. Lyme disease is very difficult to determine. This is because the symptoms are so varied and because they can occur so long after the tick bite. Antibiotics kill the bacterium causing Lyme disease. If they are not given early enough, however, permanent damage can occur.

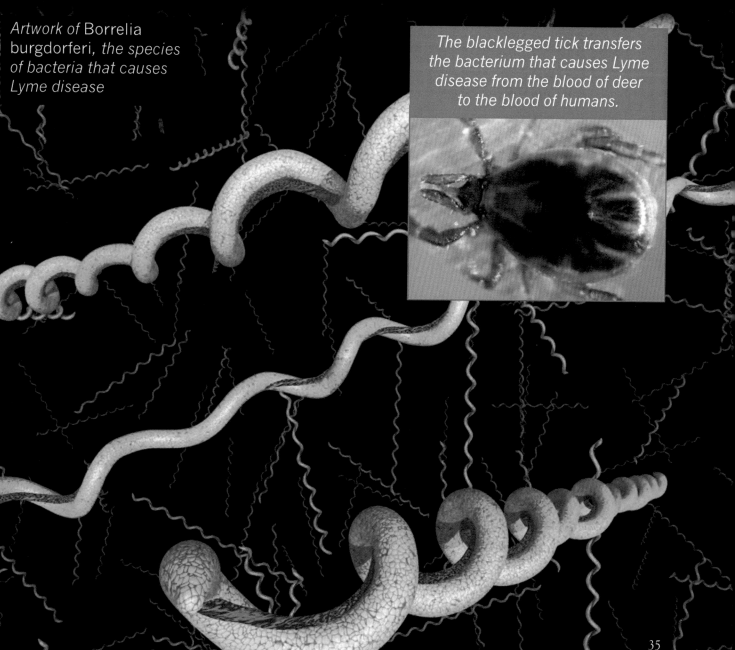

Artwork of Borrelia burgdorferi, *the species of bacteria that causes Lyme disease*

The blacklegged tick transfers the bacterium that causes Lyme disease from the blood of deer to the blood of humans.

Curved Bacteria and Stomach Problems

Two spirilla are famous for causing human disease. *Helicobacter pylori* (commonly known as *H. pylori*) is unusual. It lives in the stomach, where the strong acids that digest food keep other bacteria away. *H. pylori* avoids the acids by living under the mucous lining of the stomach wall. Here it is protected. It also produces chemicals that cancel out the acids around it. *H. pylori* is found in about 30 percent of people. It is a leading cause of stomach ulcers and stomach cancer. It can be treated with antibiotics. *Campylobacter* causes nausea, vomiting, and diarrhea. In fact, it is the leading cause of diarrhea worldwide. It is transferred to people through uncooked meat or shrimp, or in water.

Flashing Lights and Mutualisms: Curved Bacteria in the Oceans

A number of fish and squid have the ability to glow. Actually, these organisms cannot glow at all, but they do house bacteria that can! Scientists do not know all the species of bacteria that have this ability, but they do know that many of them are comma-shaped species in the genus *Vibrio*. Several kinds of fish and squid living in both shallow and deep oceans have glowing organs. The Hawaiian bobtail squid *Euprymna scolopes* lives in shallow waters off the coasts of Hawaii. This squid has two small, bright lights on either side of its body. The lights are glowing *Vibrio fischeri*. Special folds in the skin of the squid form a cavity where the bacteria live. The squid provides food, and the bacterium provides light. The squid uses the lights as camouflage by matching its glow to moonlight and shines it on the sea floor. This prevents prey from seeing its shadow, so they do not know it is approaching.

CHOLERA

Vibrio cholerae is a comma-shaped bacterium. It causes cholera, which is a serious diarrhea that can kill. The bacterium is found in water, particularly in countries around the world without water treatment. Death can happen very quickly—in a matter of hours or days. The disease is so severe because the bacterium releases a poison that makes the body's cells pump their water out into the intestines. The extreme, sudden loss of water all over the body causes shock. Cholera is rare in North America. This is because the bacterium is destroyed by water treatment that is common in most communities.

International Medical Corps officers hand out water purification equipment and give water health and hygiene information to children in Iraqi cities in a drive to prevent cholera outbreaks.

Vibrio Species: Toxic Sushi

The meat of puffer fish is eaten raw in Japan. This delicacy can cost as much as $200 U.S. for a single meal. Eating puffer fish meat is dangerous, as the fish have a powerful poison in their organs. If some of the poison from the organs gets on the meat, the person who eats it could be dead in as little as 20 minutes. The poison, TTX, is more than 1,000 times more powerful than cyanide. It causes the nerves to stop working, and the victim is paralyzed. Deaths occur in Japan every year from eating puffer fish, even though only specially trained chefs are allowed to prepare it.

A plate of fugu sashimi—thinly sliced pieces of raw puffer fish

Puffer fish poison does not come from the puffer fish itself, but the bacteria living in its intestines. Species of *Vibrio* are the most common puffer fish poison producers. A few rod-shaped bacteria also produce the same poison. The *Vibrio* bacteria live in the fish's gut, where they are safe and have food. The fish absorbs the poison the bacteria makes into its organs. The puffer fish is immune to the poison, but its predators are not. Most of them stay well away!

The highly toxic torafugu is one puffer fish used to make the Japanese dish fugu (Japanese for "puffer fish").

Deep-sea anglerfish also rely on glowing bacteria to catch their food. Some of these monstrous-looking fish have a long tube on top of their heads, with a glowing ball at the end. The tube hangs in front of their heads, like a fishing pole. The glowing ball attracts animals looking for something to eat. The anglerfish waits until the prey is close enough to its large mouth, then it grabs it with its big teeth. Each species of anglerfish with a glowing ball has its own species of glowing bacterium. The bacteria are related to *Vibrio* but have never been grown in the laboratory, so not much else is known about them.

All glowing bacteria make their glow in the same way. A chemical the bacteria produces is brought into contact with oxygen. The chemical reacts with the oxygen, and light is given off. The light can be white, green, blue, or yellow, depending on the bacteria species and the chemical. No individual bacteria produce light. They only do so when they are living with many other individuals of their species.

Hot Springs Symbionts

Some curved bacteria are important symbionts of organisms that live around holes in the ocean floor, where hot water sprays out into the open ocean. Known as hydrothermal vents, these underwater "hot springs" have an amazing variety of life. Giant tubeworms, clams, and shrimp live here. Many of these organisms have species of bacteria living in them that provide them with nutrition, and some of these bacteria are curved. Tubeworms do not have a mouth or any guts. They cannot feed on their own. The billions of bacteria that live inside their bodies provide them with all their nutrition. In return, the bacteria are provided with a safe place to live, as well as hydrogen sulfide (rotten egg gas), which the bacteria use to make energy.

A deep-sea anglerfish uses its "fishing pole" appendage and glowing ball to attract prey.

CASE STUDY

Vibrio harveyi:
The Mystery of the Milky Sea

Legend has it that on dark, summer nights on the Indian Sea, sailors can find themselves sailing on a mysterious milky sea. Witnesses to this rare event describe a dark sky with an eerie ocean that looks like glowing milk, all the way to the horizon. Satellite images showing large regions of the ocean glowing intensely have proven that these legends are true.

Some scientists think milky sea is caused by large numbers of glowing *Vibrio harveyi* bacteria. It is a mystery why such large numbers of the bacteria would occur in one place, however. Milky sea happens during the summer, which is the time when algae grow in large numbers. Perhaps there are so many bacteria in one place because they are feeding on dead and dying algae? To test the idea, researchers collected samples of milky sea and identified the species present. They found dead algae and *V. harveyi*, but not in large enough numbers to make them glow. Glowing bacteria are still the most likely explanation for the milky sea, but it hasn't been proven yet. It remains a mystery...for now.

The rare event of milky sea has been captured by satellite photography. The large area of glowing ocean, which is located just off the Horn of Africa, is big enough to be seen from space! This computer generated artwork shows the size of the area of milky sea.

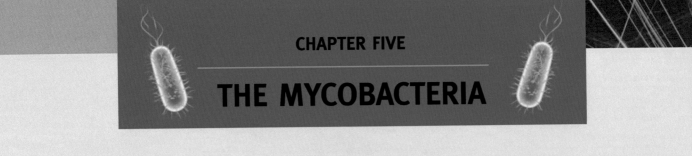

CHAPTER FIVE

THE MYCOBACTERIA

Mycobacteria are rod-shaped but have a distinct, thick cell wall that sets them apart from other groups. Their cell wall also protects them from chemicals and other outside elements, including antibiotics.

A Waxy Wall of Protection

Myco means "wax" in Greek, and the cell wall is composed of waxy substances. It is thus water repellent. The cell wall also resists gram staining. Other, more complicated staining techniques must be used to see them. These bacteria are called "acid fast." This is because acids that are applied during the staining process do not affect the cells. There are very few acid-fast cells known, so the trait is very useful in identifying the group.

Mycobacteria are aerobic and lack flagella, so they generally do not move of their own accord. They are also slow growing. Some mycobacteria live in soil and water as decomposers. Other species live on animals, causing no harm. A few cause disease.

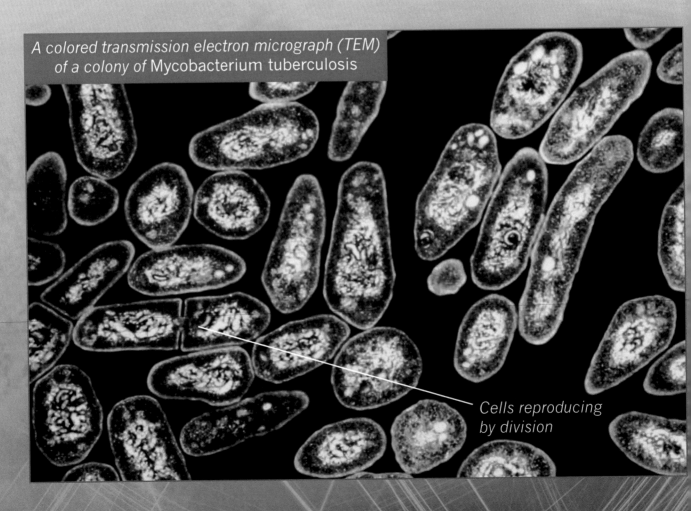

A colored transmission electron micrograph (TEM) of a colony of Mycobacterium tuberculosis

Cells reproducing by division

Difficult to Kill

The waxy cell wall on mycobacteria protects them, and they are difficult to destroy. Species that live in tap water are unaffected by chlorine treatment, and most antibiotics do them little harm. The immune system also has a difficult time destroying them, because the cell wall is difficult to break down. The several species that cause disease in humans are thus particularly dangerous. Two mycobacteria are famous for the suffering and death they have caused: *Mycobacterium tuberculosis*, the cause of tuberculosis; and *Mycobacterium leprae,* the cause of leprosy.

Tuberculosis: A Bacterium of Historic Proportions

Tuberculosis, or TB for short, infects about one-third of the world's population at any one time. In 90–95 percent of these people, it does not cause any illness. Most people with the bacterium do not know they have it, and they cannot spread it to others. Enough people with the bacterium do become ill, however, for TB to be the leading cause of death by any parasite. It has killed more people over the course of history than all wars put together.

In the most common form of TB, the bacteria live inside the white blood cells of the lungs, the body's first defense. Not only does this bacterium resist the immune system, it also destroys it. In the process, lung tissue is damaged. TB is a slow disease, as more and more lung tissue is damaged. In many patients, the immune system gets the infection under control before the victim is sick enough to die. In some, though, the bacterium spreads through the entire lungs, or to other places throughout the body, and the victim dies.

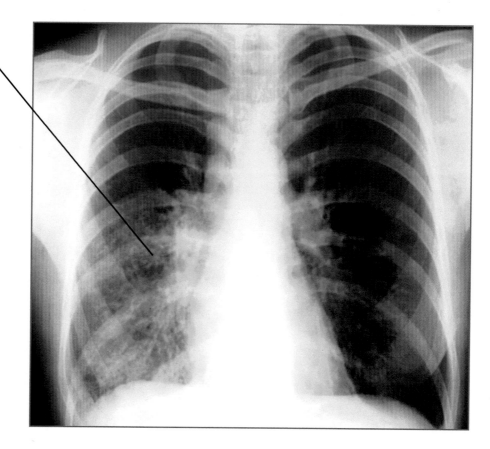

A colored chest X-ray of a woman with pulmonary tuberculosis (red areas) in her lungs

A white blood cell (shown in green) engulfs bacteria (shown in orange) introduced into the body with the tuberculosis vaccine. The bacteria are live but weakened. They prime the body's immune system without causing disease, so the immune system responds more rapidly if infected with tuberculosis bacteria in the future.

Mycobacterium tuberculosis: Treatment by Prevention

There has been a vaccine for TB since the 1920s. It is made from *Mycobacterium bovis* (*M. bovis*), which causes tuberculosis in cows. The bacterium used in the vaccine has been genetically changed so it is weak and does not cause disease. Since the late 1980s, however, the vaccine has been losing its ability to prevent the form of TB that targets the lungs. Because it still prevents other forms of TB illness, it is given to 100 million newborn children every year worldwide. There is currently no protection against the main form of the disease, however, and the form of TB that targets the lungs still kills three million people every year.

In 2009, scientists discovered the reason the vaccine stopped working. The bacterium used in the vaccine increased the production of chemicals that protect *M. bovis* from the body's immune response. So when the vaccine is injected, there is no immune response and no future protection against the bacterium. Now that scientists understand why the vaccine no longer works, they are planning to change the bacterium back to a form that does cause an immune response. There is hope that in the years to come, TB will no longer cause so many deaths.

Leprosy: An Ancient Enemy

Leprosy has been recognized as a disease for thousands of years. It causes damage to the skin and nerves. Today it is commonly known as Hansen's disease, after G. H. A. Hansen, the scientist who in the late 1800s discovered *Mycobacterium leprae.* The bacterium lives in nerve cells in the skin, destroying them. Though it takes years for the disease to develop, with symptoms beginning as long as 20 years after infection, the disease causes distorted features and patches of dead, rotting tissue. Over time, the patches of dead tissue get bigger, there is damage to the limbs and face, and the victim becomes disabled.

Throughout history, people with leprosy have been forced to live separately, walk in separate places, and wear special clothing to warn others of their presence. Today, there are fewer cases of Hansen's disease. Three drugs given in combination cure the disease, and the World Health Organization gives these drugs at no charge to all identified patients in the world. An estimated 14 million people have been cured so far. The effort is continuing.

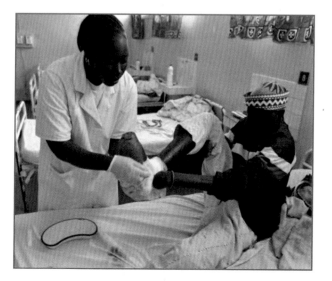

A nurse dresses the wounds of a young man with leprosy at the Applied Leprosy Research Institute in Daka, Senegal.

Glossary

antibiotic A substance produced by a microorganism that kills other microorganisms; antibiotics are used heavily in medicine to treat bacterial infections

autotroph An organism that obtains its carbohydrate nutrients (sugars and starches) from chemical reactions involving a source of energy in the environment, usually the Sun

***Bacillus* (plural *Bacilli*)** Rod-shaped bacteria; also a particular genus of rod-shaped bacteria

binary fission The means by which bacteria replicate; the cell contents are doubled, a cell wall forms down the middle, and then the cell splits apart to form two identical cells

biofilm A complex mat of many species of bacteria and other microorganisms that develops on a solid surface, such as a plant, plastic (under water), or teeth

cell The smallest unit of life

classification The method scientists use to name and organize organisms into groups

coccus (plural *cocci*) Round- or oval-shaped bacteria

diarrhea Abnormally frequent and watery bowel movements

DNA Deoxyribonucleic acid, a complex molecule that is the blueprint for life, which contains all the "instructions" for building cells; organisms reproduce by replicating their DNA

dormant Alive but not actively growing; in a slowed-down state

eukaryotic Having to do with organisms that have a nucleus and other cell parts separated from the rest of the cell by a membrane; plants, animals, fungi, and protists are eukaryotes

feces The solid waste that is removed from the body during a bowel movement

flagellum (plural *flagella*) A long, thin, whip-like structure that projects from some bacteria and is used for movement

gene A segment of DNA that carries the information for a particular trait or the making of a particular protein

genus A group of closely related species

heterotroph An organism that obtains its nutrients (sugars and starches) from other organisms, dead or alive

immune system An animal's defenses against parasites and disease

infection The presence of disease-causing organisms

insulin A hormone that regulates the amount of glucose, or sugar, in the blood; the lack of insulin causes a form of diabetes

lactic acid A syrupy organic acid formed in sour milk and produced by the muscles during exercise

membrane A thin layer that acts as a barrier between cell parts or between a cell and the environment

molecule A grouping of two or more atoms bonded together; the smallest unit of a chemical compound that can take part in a chemical reaction

mutualist An organism—or having to do with organisms—living in a symbiotic association that benefits both organisms

nucleus (plural *nuclei*) The part of the cell where DNA is located

nutrients Molecules used by the body for growth, repair, and reproduction

organism A living being; can refer to an individual or a species

paralyze The loss of motion and feeling in the body as a result of nerves and/or muscles not working

parasite A species that lives in a relationship with another species in which the host is harmed

plasmid A small ring of DNA that is found free within the cell of bacteria; plasmid DNA does not include instructions that are necessary for life

prokaryotic Having to do with unicellular organisms whose cells do not have a nucleus or other cell parts that are separated from the rest of the cell by a membrane; bacteria and archaea are prokaryotes

pus A white, gooey substance that consists of bacteria cells and live and dead white blood cells; pus is found at the site of infection and indicates that the body's immune system is working to rid the body of bacteria

resistance The ability of an organism to survive exposure to a substance that once killed it; resistance occurs because a change in genes gives individuals the new survival ability

ribosome The site in a cell where proteins are made based on the instructions contained in genes

rumen The large compartment of the stomach of cows, sheep, and related animals; the site where cellulose is broken down by bacteria and other microorganisms

saprotrophs Organisms that obtain their carbohydrate nutrients (sugars and starches) from dead organisms; saprotrophs decompose organisms

species A group of individual organisms that has so many of the same genes that they are able to mate and exchange DNA

spirillum (plural *spirilla*) Spiral-shaped bacteria; as *Spirillum*, a genus of spiral-shaped bacteria

spirochete A genetically related group of bacteria that have a long, twisty shape

Staphylococcus **(plural *Staphylococci*)** Round-shaped bacteria that occur in clusters; also a particular genus of bacteria with this arrangement

Streptobacillus **(plural *Streptobacilli*)** Rod-shaped bacteria that occur in rows; also a particular genus of bacteria with this arrangement

Streptococcus **(plural *Streptococci*)** Round-shaped bacteria that occur in chains; also a particular genus of bacteria with this arrangement

symptom Evidence of physical disease or disturbance as noticed by the patient

vaccine A preparation of the dead cells, parts of cells, or genetically altered cells of bacteria (or viruses) that is given to people in order to prepare their immune systems and protect them from the disease in the future

Vibrio Comma-shaped bacteria; also a particular genus of bacteria with this shape

virus Any of a large group of particles with DNA that infect cells causing disease; viruses cannot grow or replicate outside living cells, and it is not clear whether they are organisms or molecules

vitamins Nutrients required in small quantities that are not used as building blocks but rather are involved in chemical reactions

white blood cells Cells of the immune system that are found in the bloodstream and find and destroy bacteria and other foreign cells that might do harm to the body

Further Information

www.cellsalive.com/toc_micro.htm
Watch *E. coli* divide, see penicillin in action, and learn how bacteria swim.

people.ku.edu/~jbrown/bugs.html
This Web site features all kinds of weird and wonderful articles on bugs in the news, including a lot of bacteria.

www.bacteriamuseum.org/
Topics at this site include evolution, food and water safety, how we fight bacteria, and bacteria in history.

www.ucmp.berkeley.edu/bacteria/bacteria.html
From the University of California Museum of Paleontology comes this site with a history of bacteria on Earth.

www.textbookofbacteriology.net
This textbook features many bacteria, with good information on a lot of diseases the organisms cause.

www.microbeworld.org/index.php
Here are plenty of interesting articles, videos, and hot news items about bacteria to keep you on this site for a long, long time.

www.livescience.com/bacteria/
Yogurt in space? Bacteria two miles underground? This site has some of the Internet's most intriguing info bytes about bacteria.

www.cdc.gov/ncidod/dbmd/diseaseinfo/foodborneinfections_g.htm
This site includes a lot of food poisoning questions and answers from the Centers for Disease Control and Prevention.

www.microbiologybytes.com/blog/tag/bacteria/
Read about what scientists who study bacteria are up to these days, and the results of their work.

Index

Index

ABOUT THE AUTHOR

Judy Wearing has been writing about science for more than ten years. She has a Ph.D. in biology from the University of Oxford and is an award-winning author and educator. Her most recent book is *Edison's Concrete Piano* (ECW Press, 2009). When not writing, Judy can be found on her hobby farm milking the goat or walking the dogs.